A gift from Bestselling Author Steve Windsor
Get access to the video tutorial bonus videos for Nine Day Novel: Self-Editing!

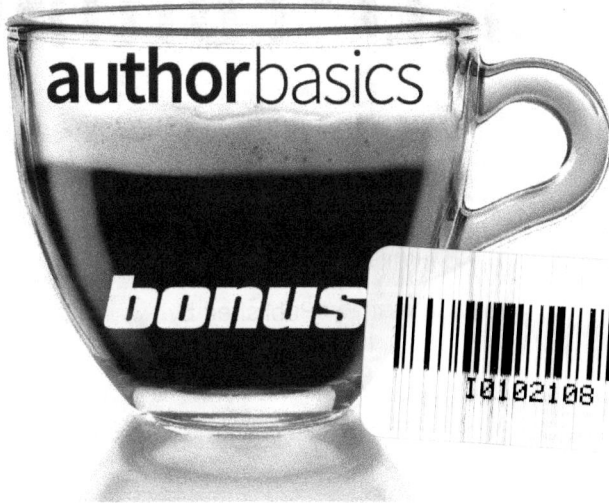

Here's how to access the bonus videos for this book.

Step 1 - Become a FREE member of Author Basics, our author training community, at https://authorbasics.com/join/

Step 2 - Visit the Nine Day Novel: Self-editing bonus blog post at https://authorbasics.com/ndn-self-editing-bonuses/

Step 3 - Enjoy the freebies!

NINE DAY NOVEL
SELF-EDITING

STEVE WINDSOR

Published by

Vixen

vixenink.com

::Disclaimer

This book is for informational purposes only.

The information found within the contents of this book may contain third-party products and services. These third-party materials consist of products and opinions expressed by their owners. As such, the author and/or the publisher do not assume responsibility or liability for any third-party material or opinions expressed.

The use of recommended third-party material does not guarantee any success and/or earnings related to you or your business. Publication of such third-party material is simply a recommendation and an expression of the author's own opinion of that particular material.

Links to third-party resources may be affiliate links, meaning the author may receive compensation if a service is ultimately purchased from such a link.

VIXEN ink

Although the author and publisher have made every effort to ensure that the information in this book was correct at press time, the author and publisher do not assume and hereby disclaim any liability to any party for any loss, damage, or disruption caused by errors or omissions, whether such errors or omissions result from negligence, accident, or any other cause.

NINE DAY NOVEL: SELF-EDITING

A VIXEN ink book/Published by arrangement with the author

Copyright © 2015 by Steve Windsor

(Printed Version)
ISBN-13: 978-0692403457
ISBN-10: 0692403450

Dedication

To all the new authors starting your journey. Use this series to help you become the author I know you can be.

Table of Contents

Foreword by Lise Cartwright

Why you need to learn to self-edit

I've always been a self-editor, and I'd expect most of you are the same. But what you probably don't know is that there is no one "right" way to edit your own novels.

However, the way Steve and I edit is a pretty good one and you *can* save yourself time, money and frustration once you hand your draft off to your editor.

Sound good? Here's how!

Read this book. Steve is my **go-to guy** when it comes to fiction. I can never remember where the ellipses go or whether it's a dash or em-dash . . . and to be honest, who really cares, right?

Well, *so* not the right attitude, because if you can nail this sort of stuff before your editor gets their hands on your book, not only will it make it easier for them to read, it'll also allow them to edit faster.

You need to get your book back in six days so you can publish it and start feeding your starving fans with your next book installment.

Did I say that *none* of this stuff excited me in the least? No? Well, it didn't, but with a little effort, it actually didn't take long to learn, and who knows, maybe one day, you won't even *need* an editor . . . (Ah, Steve, you might wanna "edit" that part out, he-he.)

Of course, that'll never happen—you need an editor.

I've read through this book several times—doing my "buddy edit"—and each time, I learn something new. I love that Steve *shows* you what he's talking about.

Examples make far more sense to me. Seeing prose and character dialogue actually happening is better than having it explained in detail.

After reading and re-reading *Nine Day Novel: Self-Editing* several times, my next plan (after I finish my first *Nine Day Novel*—I keep telling Steve he's insane, but he's dragging me to the water) is to apply what I've learned and then write another book! I'm going to have *NDN: Writing* and *NDN: Editing* right beside me every step of the way.

And if I can suck it up and learn this stuff, you can too.

If you want to be a serious, **profitable fiction writer**, then you need skills. That's what I love about Steve's books—they're practical application of so much theory that I can't stand reading.

With his help, I guarantee you'll get that novel done, proofed and handed to your editor fast.

So without further ado, turn the page and "go learn things," as Dwayne Pride (*NCIS: New Orleans*) always says.

Lise Cartwright
Best-selling author and fiction virgin

NINE DAY NOVEL: SELF-EDIT-ING

EDITING BASICS

CONGRATULATIONS!

Congratulations!

You just finished the draft of your first novel!

"What do I do next?" If you're like I was, that was the first question you asked yourself after typing the last of those 50,000-plus words.

I actually wrote this book to solve that problem for myself . . . once and for all my future novels. But first, I had to ask myself another question. **Did I write a good story?** (Actually a big part of editing.)

If you've already read *Nine Day Novel: Writing*, in your story, you ran your hero ragged through the Four Part Story Structure (4PSS). He or she either triumphed over evil, found love, or you struck him or her down in a blaze of glory so satisfying that it was okay for your hero to be martyred for the cause.

If you did that, then yahoo! Now your novel's ready for your adoring fans, right? Uh, we're not *quite* there yet.

Do you remember what I said last time?

Steve, I totally remember: You said after every one of those examples that once we finished writing it was, "Bravo! Pop champagne and. . ."

Oh, you *do* remember. You remember that little part *after* the champagne about calling someone, right? And that person was. . .?

Your Editor—the Last Line of Defense

But editors cost a lot of money, and wouldn't it be helpful if we could minimize some of that expense by doing a bit of editing ourselves before we send our draft to them?

But I'm a writer, I don't know how to edit.

That's what I said the first time I was faced with the prospect of paying an editor to clean up my draft. But with some painful trial and error, some great tools, and a few lessons in the basics of writing fiction, I've since saved hundreds on expensive deep edits of my novels.

Don't make the mistake I did!

On my very first novel, I debated for months between paying for what is arguably the most costly part of self-publishing a novel, and whether I should just "edit" the entire thing myself. After all, how hard could it be?

Predictably, money won out, and I chose poorly, publishing my first novel before a professional editor had proofread it.

Big mistake. That one decision set my writing career back about a year.

Why? Because my book, *Cramdown*, languished on Amazon as yet another unprofessional, unfinished and unwanted draft, posing as a finished novel. Luckily I pulled it before any damage could be done.

But there *was* damage. I got discouraged, disappointed and down. It took months before I overcame my fear of what a professional editor would say about my first novel. Because that was the *real* reason I had edited it myself all along.

A great editor will make your novel shine. You need one . . . for more reasons than you think.

Picture your reader, trying to follow the fantastic story that you painstakingly outlined, researched and wrote. As they read, their eyes are interrupted by misspellings, grammatical errors, improper word usage and dialogue that's punctuated poorly. Finally, unable to stay engaged through those constant interruptions, they give up and close your book. Or worse, they decide to leave you a bad review.

We're not going to let that happen!

Next to your book cover, your editor will have the single biggest impact on the professional look and feel of your novel. But that doesn't mean we can't do a little bit of "editing" ourselves. In fact, inside this book, I'll show you how you can do quite a bit of it before your draft needs to go to an editor.

And that's gonna save you money. One thing that's in short supply for many of us self-published authors.

Editing for Writers

By showing you the basics of how to write fiction sentences correctly and efficiently in the first place, you'll learn how to speed up your self-edits at the end of your draft.

I'll help you minimize mistakes while you write by covering the following things:

- The basics of punctuating fiction

- "Tricks" you can use to make your novels more reader friendly
- How to "edit" as you go
- How to write thought
- Writing sound
- And more. . .

Removing the mystery

To many beginning authors, editing is a mysterious and often misunderstood process.

In this book, I'll define the types of editing you need, outline the parts that you can and should do yourself, and then explain the process that your editor will go through as they clean up your final draft.

No idea where to find a great editor? I'll show you how to find one on popular freelancing sites. Exactly what to say to them and what type of edit you need them to do.

Still nervous? I'll give you the contact information of my own editor. She's awesome!

And I'll introduce you to a piece of software that'll save you countless hours, working with your editor.

I'll walk you through the steps my writing partner and I

use to fix our own drafts before we ship them to our editor.

- The right way to use your spell-checker
- Step-by-step proofreading your entire draft
- How to get rid of Word's "track changes" function forever
- How to find a good editor on popular free-lancing sites
- How to get your editor to edit your draft directly

Editing is much easier if you don't make mistakes in the first place.

Seems simple, right? It should be.

For that reason, I felt it was important for this book to have two parts to it: How to clean up what you had already written . . . and how to minimize all that cleanup by knowing what and how to write fiction sentences in the first place.

This book is split into two parts

The first half of the book is the editing process, procedures, and workflow we use to self-edit our own novels and collaborate with our editors in real time. And the second half is a refresher course on the very basics of writing fiction sentences.

So whether you've never worked with an editor before or you just want to save some time, money and headache, editing your next draft, **I wrote this book for you!**

Nine Day Novel Series

I wrote the *Nine Day Novel* series to help beginning and up-and-coming fiction authors navigate the information and basic skills they'll need in order to successfully start the journey to becoming published authors.

These books aren't end-all be-all guides to everything fiction writing. They're how-to books about the basics. They contain my experiences on what works well . . . for me.

In addition, as those of you who've read *NDN: Writing* know, I don't like slow and steady. That book was about a format and schedule to help you structure your novel and write the ***first draft*** in nine days . . . literally.

I wanted to give you the motivation to finish what I see so many unable to do!

This book is another tool in the series to **help you clean**

that draft up. More importantly, make sure there weren't as many mistakes in the first place.

Who We Are

I have a great author friend, Lise Cartwright. I told you about her in the *NDN: Writing* book.

As your writing career progresses, you'll find your team —fellow writers who work like you do and challenge you to do more. It helps if they're a bit better than you are at some things, so they push you to rise to greater heights in a particular area. And you need to push them where you're strong.

And, lest we get too far off the rails of the subject of this book, you need **a writing partner who's willing to do a thorough read-through of your draft—a "Buddy Edit."**

Give back.

The independent author community is growing fast and we all have common needs and challenges. One of our biggest, is overcoming obscurity. Luckily there are people who can help.

QUICK TIP:
Buck Books is a great service for indie authors to promote their books. You can sign up to get emailed about their FREE and $0.99 book promotions HERE. Or you can sign up as an affiliate to submit your books for promotion HERE.

Shhh. . . There are no secrets.

I don't have any secrets. I put in the hours.

Even the "secrets" that I find out about as I consume massive amounts of advice from other authors who are ahead of me in their careers. . . People who don't always agree, mind you.

What I've found is that there aren't really secrets, only further insight. And anyone can use that insight as long as they're willing to do the "Darth"—clash lightsabers with the hard work.

Write better, edit less.

When I first set out to write fiction, I had no idea what I was doing. So I read everything I could. I mean, what do you write down as your first sentence if you've never written a single word of fiction?

All the advice I found started in the middle—how to make dialogue sound cool and flow. Or something cryptic like "show, don't tell."

But I wanted to know how to *write* it. What dialogue looked like . . . physically? Not how to make it cool. I knew that would take practice and finding my "voice." No one can do that for you.

So I started with the basics.

The second half of this book

What I *can* show you, after scouring all of that information, is where a comma, an ellipsis, an em-dash, quotes, and question marks go . . . exactly. Then you can use that information to develop your own writing style. More importantly, your reader can read what you write without being interrupted, trying to figure out who said what, when, where and to whom.

And what does all that have to do with editing? Or, more importantly, *self*-editing before you ever send your draft to an editor? A lot.

Make it clean, then give it to the professionals.

I can't quote the Chicago Manual of Style, and I have to look up how AP style suggests using an ellipsis, but I can tell you what I've learned. After reading and researching all of the author how-to materials I can get my hands on about how to punctuate, format, organize and proofread your own works: **No one agrees**.

In the real fiction writing world, one author uses em-dashes to the extreme instead of commas and another won't even think of using an ellipsis because he says it makes his characters sound wimpy, trailing off speech all the time.

So we aren't going there. I'm going to show you examples of what you *can* do to make sure that, as you write, your draft is as clean as possible before you start self-editing.

WISK (This is my "When I'm Stephen King" quote section from the last time.)

"Badges? We don't need no stinking badges." - *Blazing Saddles*

Here's my version:
"Motivation? I don't need no stinking motivation. I need

information!"

This isn't a book on how to motivate yourself.

In *NDN: Writing,* I warmed you up with some techniques, tips and tactics I use to carve out time to write, and then get the words on the page any way you have to, making sure that you adhere to the Four Part Story Structure that we discussed in that book.

If you're serious about being a paid author, then writing isn't only a calling, a dream, a passion, a precious wish you had one day. . . This here . . . this be a J.O.B., baby. One that you will love, to be sure, but one that'll make you earn that love . . . in labor.

If you need a little "motivation" to get down to business. . .

Slap yourself across the face with some coffee, do a jumping jack, kick everyone out of your room and let's get some work done!

RESOURCES

Links in the Book

Throughout this book you'll find links to books, author pages and software. Some of these are affiliate links and I make a little money if you buy something.

I'll also refer to different resources—software and services—Lise and I use to edit more efficiently.

Here they are. (I'm only going to link to these here.)

Scrivener—the best writing program I've found for mind-mapping, outlining, organizing, writing, editing, formatting and self-publishing. (I put a quick 10-minute video on Scrivener basics in the bonus content.)

Dropbox—an online cloud storage service. Keep your files there, sync them to your local computer, and then access them from anywhere. (Also, it's how Lise and I share our Scrivener files with each other and our editors.

It's the example I'll be using in this book.)

If you skipped the bonus offer page at the start of this book, here's how you access the bonus videos.

Step 1 - become a FREE member of Author Basics at https://authorbasics.com/join

Step 2 - Visit the Nine Day Novel: Self-editing bonus blog post at https://authorbasics.com/ndn-self-editing-bonuses/

In the videos, I'll show you specific functions inside Scrivener that you can use in order to edit directly inside that program. Tutorial videos detailing how we edit, share, and back up our Scrivener project files—our books.

Also, in *NDN: Writing,* I offered access to the Scrivener 4PSS Starter File containing all the parts of the Four Part Story Structure (4PSS) as chapters and documents to help you outline. (It's available as a Word .doc as well.) I'll reference that file inside this book.

WHAT YOU CAN EXPECT

The "WISK" Section . . . from last time

We're going to stick with the "This was going to be Stephen King quotes about writing section" that I hijacked in the last book.

So, since the King isn't returning my calls, I'm continuing to use my own quotes. Presumptuous, yes, but my butt's in the seat writing, so I'm doing it. My quote section —"When I'm Stephen King"—WISK.

My Writer "Voice"

I got a lot of great feedback in reviews of the Nine Day Novel series. *Most* of them liked the voice and style I use and my "cut to the chase" pace in the books. So "No need to mess with what ain't broke," my daddy used to say.

"Darth Vader" will be back for his return appearance. Better learn to swing that lightsaber, Luke.

The "QUICK TIP" Section

This area offers helpful hints and pitfalls to avoid, and any other tidbits of information that are useful at that point.

Do What Works

Throughout this entire fiction writing basics series, and the way I do just about everything, I have a mantra, motto, "moronic" way of thinking, I don't care what you call it. . . This is my advice to you as a new, struggling and yet to be as successful as you want to be writer: Start with the basics and. . .

Do what works for you.

I wanted to pack this series of books full of real-world, real examples—the basics of writing and publishing fiction novels as an indie author.

If you liked *NDN: Writing*, it was probably because it got you motivated to put words on the page that you could see. A tangible ***first draft*** that followed the Four Part Story Structure that you could hold in your hands.

You gotta have a little fun.

In that book I used a lot of . . . tongue-in-cheek "family-abandonment" time management suggestions that some people took a little too seriously.

The spirit of it was to show you that you don't have to stick to conventional wisdom—you *can* write a novel by being super focused for short periods of time, instead of pacing yourself for years with no results.

The way I write isn't for everyone—it's just one way in many. So use the insight and find *your* way.

Rest assured, I'm still alive, my wife and kids still know what I look like . . . and I've written, edited and published several novels and non-fiction titles in short bursts of time. It can be done.

WHY YOU NEED AN EDITOR

WISK

"Editor? Do I have to? Oh, you're *so* getting an editor!"

Why You Need a Pro

When I first started writing, I wrote insanely huge novels. I still have to go back and fix them.

My first project was a sci-fi series that ended up with something like 30-40 characters all converging to a final destination. I wrote almost 250,000 words for each of two books, and had to go back through and chop them down to a more manageable 150,000. *That* . . . was difficult editing. I must have read through that first book five times, chopping and cutting and slicing all my "beautiful" words.

And you know what happened? I decided that I'd been through it so many times, that it didn't need an editor. The truth was, at the time, I didn't want to *pay* for an editor.

So I packaged it, self-published it on Kindle and Create-Space, and ordered a copy. When I got the proof back, it was riddled with errors. I was simply too close to my book —knew the story too well—to be able to do it myself. Forget the fact that I didn't have the skills necessary to fully edit anyone's book, much less my own.

So now, I get a draft as close as possible, adhering to the sentence and punctuation guidelines I'll show you later, and then I negotiate price with my editor based on word count and how "clean" the book is, and then I hand it off.

QUICK TIP:
Most editors have a per-word rate sheet based on word count and turnaround time. The rate can also take into account the type of editing required (proofreading, basic edit, substantive, developmental, etc.). Ask them for this sheet. They should be happy to provide it to you.

Finding an Editor

Follow these tips on how to find a great editor to work with:

Price

You can find reasonably-priced editors on outsourcing sites like oDesk or Elance (Now Upwork).

Make sure you're explicit about what you're looking for in your editor. This means spelling out that you want your draft proofread and also stating what you don't want them to do.

You should include strict timelines about when you need the manuscript back. And be sure to state if you want the price to include any further edits after you've reviewed changes.

What to look for

If you're sourcing an editor on Fiverr, only work with those who have a high rating and good feedback. Don't opt to work with a new editor. This isn't the time to give someone a shot at editing your novel as they learn.

Again, make sure that timelines and requirements are explicitly communicated to them. In most instances, when you purchase the "gig," they'll tell you how long it'll take for the editor to get back to you.

If you need to change that timeline or want something faster, I'd recommend that you contact the editor *before* you purchase their gig. You can contact any seller on Fiverr by viewing their profile and then clicking on the "contact me" below their profile image and bio.

In both instances, you also need to make sure that the editor can reach out to you if they need to clarify anything. Either share your Skype details with them or be open to communicating on the platform you've hired them through. Direct emails are often not allowed, so keep this in mind as well.

Use Your Personal Network.

The other option of sourcing an editor is to reach out to your other author friends and find out if they can provide you with a recommendation. Check any Facebook groups you belong to or your "friends" on Goodreads. These are both good places to start.

Whatever option you choose, make sure you're happy with what they're going to provide. You could get them to do a paid trial, where you give them the first chapter. This will help you see if they're the editor you're looking for.

Sample Pages

As we mentioned, have some sample pages—maybe

500 to 1,000 words—that represent your work, so that an editor can work on them and give you an idea of how they would edit your document.

QUICK TIPS:
Before you hire an editor, you should be clear on:

- Your budget
- The level of editing you want
- Your word count
- Turnaround time
- How busy an editor is

Wherever you find an editor, you're creating a professional relationship with them that you want to last. Continually evaluate that to make sure that it's mutually beneficial. You may need to try a couple of different editors before you find "yours."

TYPES OF EDITING

I'll explain these in reverse order from the way editing is normally done. Light to deep. The reason for that is that we need to address the deeper substantive parts when we outline and write our story.

Proofreading

Proofreading's normally the final step in editing. Someone corrects overlooked errors at the very end. It's a final read-through before you click that "submit" button.

In our world, this is something that your personal read-through and your writing buddy's read-through will do.

Copyediting

Copyediting is reading through each sentence carefully, looking for spelling, punctuation, capitalization, grammar, and word usage errors.

It's not, altering your writer "voice" or story. In a copy edit, you rewrite incorrect sentence structure and improper word usage or meaning.

Developmental

A developmental edit helps you with concept, outlining and story development. We should do most of this before we start writing as part of creating our outline and story structure.

A developmental editor *can* help you figure out what story you're going to tell, but that type of edit is more expensive.

For us independent self-published authors, developing our story is largely up to us. We need to make sure we create a story that fits within the Four Part Story Structure, and then write to that outline.

Your writing partner can help you, but you should test your own story's plot points against the 4PSS as you outline it.

Substantive

A substantive edit is a deep analytical review that checks for readability, accuracy and consistency. A substantive editor finds inconsistencies in your story, characters, or the voice you use for each person in your story. It checks to see if your plot makes sense. It can also include sentence and paragraph fixes, and major additions or subtractions to your prose.

Once again—though now you can at least speak from a place of understanding—most of what we do as indie authors is copyediting and proofing after our novel is written.

QUICK TIP:
Story development, character consistency, and plot checking are expensive edits. Cut down on that cost by studying story structure, sentence structure and dialogue punctuation, and practicing all the time by writing more.

Self-Editing

Copyediting and proofreading it yourself

This is simply the start-to-finish spelling and grammar check that we performed with our software's spell-checker. After that, we perform our full read-through—line by line, sentence by sentence, checking for mistakes in dialogue punctuation, misused words, and spelling and grammar errors that the built-in spell-checkers don't catch.

QUICK TIP:

Make sure you read slowly enough that your eyes and brain don't skip over sentences or words. As familiar as you are with your story, your mind knows what's coming and has a tendency to skip ahead.

This is why many suggest that you read your entire draft out loud. It's painful, but it works.

You can combine this with a technique that some authors and editors use—starting at the back of your novel and reading sentence by sentence to the beginning. I tried it a few times and did find errors, but it's brutally boring.

Developmental/substantive self-edit

We need to make sure we've outlined and vetted a good story before we ever start writing. Follow the steps that were outlined in *NDN: Writing* to develop a high-concept story that contains all of the major milestones in the Four Part Story Structure. By doing that, we'll avoid hiring an editor to perform this deep edit ourselves.

Our writing partner's read-through will help us with this by pointing out any inconsistencies, confusion or missing information from their unbiased—unfamiliar with our story —point of view. It may or may not be a deep substantive edit, but it'll be good enough. And that'll be our sanity check.

Gut check

The combination of a developmental and substantive edit should answer these questions:

- Do you feel like your story makes sense?
- Does your story conform to the Four Part Story Structure?
- Have you checked it for inconsistencies in character actions, incorrect information or

confusing sections?

- In short, can a reader who's not familiar with your story get engaged and understand it? (This can only be determined with the help of that outside reader.)

THE "RIGHT" WAY

WISK

"However you get it done . . . that's the 'right' way."

There's no "right" way to edit.

The workflow and suggestions I suggest work for me, but you may find only pieces of it work for you. Everyone is different. Adapt the ideas in this book—any book for that matter—to fit your needs.

Example:
Here's one way to edit your novel. Write it four times? Ouch. Here's what they suggest.

Round 1—Write a day's worth of work. We know what that means from *NDN: Writing*—10 hours, 5,000-10,000 words. The next day, *before* you write anything else, edit the previous day's work. What? I'm *writing* on that day . . . until day nine! (You already know this is blasphemy from my point of view as I just want the draft finished, then I'll turn around and edit it.) This is "**Darth Interrupted.**"

Round 2—Once your first draft's complete, go back to the beginning and edit the entire draft. They call it the "close-in edit," and it becomes your second draft—the second time you "write" your book. Ugh! **"Darth's in the Details."**

Round 3—**Print it out and read it . . . again**. (*OMG!* This is making me scream.) Take notes, scribble, whatever. Then, take those notes and go back and make the changes you scribbled notes about. Now you've "written" your book three times. I call this one **"Darth Death to Trees."**

Round 4—Read it out loud. This one's actually great advice and a lot of people give it. I've tried it. You'll need 12 hours and a serious amount of coffee to get you through it. Read every word out loud until you're done. Let's call it . . . **"Darth Diatribe"** or "DD"—Dammit, I'm so Done!

Then you *are* done. Why? Because you aren't going to do all that, are you? Bet your bootie you aren't gonna do it, because it's painful.

So, let's see what we can do to eliminate one or two of those four. We *will* have to read through our novel to proof it, but not four times.

FIRING WORD

Editing . . . for writers

"Ah, now eventually you do plan to have *dinosaurs* on your . . . on your dinosaur tour, right?" - Dr. Ian Malcolm, *Jurassic Park*

WISK

"Steve, when do we get to the editing part? Uh, yeah, I'm getting there."

Cutting Word Loose

After too many hours spent exporting and importing drafts, cutting and pasting back and forth from Scrivener to Word and back again, I made a decision to cut Word loose for good. Now, I edit right inside Scrivener. Lise does too.

Any editing job we post to find an editor, our major requirement is familiarity with and willingness to edit directly inside Scrivener.

We tested this strategy ourselves before we unleashed it on our editors. I simply closed myself out of the Scrivener project file that we kept in a shared Dropbox folder, and Lise opened it. Then she proofread through it and made changes. When she was done, she closed it and then I opened the file back up and skimmed through it, "accepting" her changes.

I think I actually said, "That's all we had to do?" Because it was so simple, and so pain-free compared to what we'd been doing, I just couldn't believe it.

There was a little more to it than that and I'll go into the details next.

QUICK TIP:

Do not format your document until it's fully edited and back from your editor, ready to publish.

Sharing your Scrivener file—if your writing buddy or editor does not have your fonts installed on their computer—will cause you to lose formatting changes. Scrivener will default to their installed fonts if it can't find the ones it needs. This will result in you having to reformat any document that your writing partner or editor changes.

Don't even ask me how I know that.

DAY 1: SPELLCHECK AND READ THROUGH

Dive In

First, I do *not* put my book down and "give it a rest" once I'm finished, as every ounce of conventional wisdom suggests.

If you *didn't* write your novel in nine days like we did in *NDN: Writing*, then chances are high that you haven't laid eyes on the beginning of your draft for weeks, months, or heaven forbid, years! So why do we want to take a break before we dive into editing it?

And before we start, hypocrite that I am, I *do* edit a tiny bit as I go. For instance, if I catch a spelling error or a double space in the line I'm working on, I'll fix it right away. It doesn't interrupt my flow and my editor and I have one less thing to worry about. So, call me out, but yes I "edit" a tiny bit as I write.

After that, this is what I do before I start and complete my editing checklist, and then give my draft to an actual professional editor.

Spelling and Grammar Check

This is simply common sense, right? You'd be amazed.

Word, Scrivener. . . Short of writing on a notepad or toilet paper, every word processor in existence has a spell-checker. Use it.

Spell-check.

Start at the very beginning and just click your way through the entire draft, addressing each and every issue that your spelling and grammar checker finds. You'll be amazed at how many errors there are. But that's what the spell-check function is for, so we're using it.

Don't trust your spell-checker.

A word of warning—your spelling and grammar checker lies like a fat dog on a porch!

Scrivener routinely tells me to use the wrong version of "there," "they're" and "their." It also confuses itself with "its" and "it's." And from a grammar perspective, anything but an Elizabethan, perfectly-structured sentence gets flagged as a "fragment."

To combat this, you'll have to go error by error, click by click through your entire draft, paying close attention to the specific error before you simply blindly accept the suggestion and hit "change." Painstaking? Yes.

This process usually takes me anywhere from 30-60 minutes, depending on how long my draft is. 90,000 words is a lot to click through.

QUICK TIP:
The "from-form" dilemma. **Pay attention to your personal typing habits and the common errors that you make.** I routinely mistype the word "from" as "form."

Typing as fast as I do, my fingers just have a habit of typing it in wrong. But will a spell-checker catch that? "Form" is a real word, so no, it won't. I have to add it to my editing checklist to find every instance of the word "form" and make sure I've used it correctly. Which gets tricky, because sometimes I actually want to use "form" and because I'm subliminally cognizant that I mess it up, I type "from."

Create a list of the common errors you make as you type and add that to your self-editing checklist.

The Read-Through

I told you we were going to use some of those four read-throughs, remember?

Do your read-through.

Sit down for some comfortable hours and "marathon" read your novel. (Or read it in the shortest period of time you can.) The reason I like to do this in one or two long stretches is that I get a little substantive edit as I go—I can think about and fix inconsistencies in my story, because the beginning will still be fresh in my mind by the time I get to the end.

Pay particular attention to punctuation and spelling and go slowly. It'll be hard because your mind knows the story, but read each word individually to catch any errors you might've missed.

The Buddy Edit

Remember when I told you to get a writing partner? Well, the very next person who'll see your draft, after you use the spell-checker and do your own read-through, is your writing buddy.

Ideally, they're another writer, but if you can get a fan, friend or family member to read it, so be it. Regardless, someone else *has* to read it.

What we want from our buddy

Set priorities with your buddy editor. If you think you only need a sanity check, say that. If you want some help with your plot points, tell them that, too. Chances are, they'll come up with a list of suggestions for you on their own, but if you're struggling in a certain area, make sure you spell that out for them before they do their read-through.

DAY 2: EDITING IN SCRIVENER

WISK

"That was just way too simple. What? I thought it would be harder than that. You wanted it to be harder?"

Our "Super Simple" Scrivener Editing Process

Okay, *nothing* is super simple, however this is how we design editing into our writing workflow:

- We outline using our own Scrivener starter file containing the Four Part Story Structure.
- We write our novel as fast as possible, adhering to the major plot milestones and sticking to that structured outline.
- We surface-edit as we go, fixing blatant spelling errors, double spaces, and dialogue tag issues in real time.
- When we're finished writing, we spell and grammar check the entire document, clicking completely through the book, fixing each error individually.
- We're careful not to trust our spell-checking

tool, because it frequently suggests incorrect changes.

- We have a list of our personal habits, errors and omissions that we check next.

- Then we perform a complete copy and proof edit at the same time, checking each sentence for errors, bad structure and awkward word pairings. This is our read-through.

- Once that's done, we take a snapshot of every document inside Scrivener (there's a video tutorial for that in the bonuses), so we can roll back to it if we don't like the changes our editor makes.

- Then we "hand off" our file in Dropbox to our buddy editor by closing out of the file, sharing it with them and letting them know it's ready.

- We share our drafts inside Dropbox for speed, convenience and backup purposes, and so we know exactly what version we're working on. (You could use Google Drive or even Microsoft One Drive.)

- Then our buddy editor opens the file and proofreads/skims the entire thing.

- Once our buddy is done with their proofread, they close out of the file and we open it and check through the entire document, accepting their changes. (There's a video tutorial in the bonuses on how we mark changes, high-light and make comments inside Scrivener.)

- We hire the best professional editor we can afford and negotiate based on word count and the cleanliness of our proofed draft.

- We have our editors work directly in Scrivener, avoiding exporting, compiling and cutting and pasting revisions from Word back into our working master file.

- Not only do we have Scrivener set up to make backups each time we exit the program, saving several revisions, but we manually back up our files before sending them to an editor.

- We share our draft Scrivener file with our editor in a Dropbox folder, so that the file never moves from its location.

- Then we "freeze" the file. (We don't touch it while the editor has it.)

While our editor is working on our file, we'll go work on an outline for another book. Or better, start submitting our book to our list of free and $0.99 book marketing sites.

Give Your Editor Six Days

Some people suggest giving the editing process two weeks. That doesn't really fit with the level of speed that we want. So to keep to our speedy timeline, I prepare my editors in advance to receive drafts and I let them know my turnaround is six days.

That usually doesn't make it more expensive—six days is reasonable turnaround time for a novel-length draft.

The Timeline

Continuing with our "nine-day" theme, on days one and two, we self-edit our own work—spell-checking, reading through and buddy-editing inside Scrivener.

On days three through eight, our editor gets access to our draft. Since we've already contacted him or her, **the next six days our draft will be in our editor's hands.**

They will complete their part of the process, ending on day eight.

So let's talk about what our editor will be doing.

DAY 3-8: WHAT YOUR EDITOR DOES

What Your Editor Wants

An editor's perspective

I asked one of our editors to list the top things she would like completed before an author sends a draft to her. So here it is, straight from one of the people you'll be working with.

I like our editor, because in addition to being awesome, she's got a slight touch of "Darth Vader" style of communication voice . . . like mine. A far gentler version, of course.

Here's her input:

1. Be open to platform. If one of us works on a Mac and the other a PC, we can work together. Just make sure I can perform the same functions you've done on your draft or can provide suitable replacements, and vice versa. (Scrivener on Mac and Windows are slightly different.)

2. Tell me your punctuation preferences. If you're a new client, a three-to-five-page sample will do. I edit those sample pages for free.

3. In editing, there are rules. We're trained to follow them, and that's a major reason you hire us. We know the regional rules, too. Or we'd better if we want to work around the world. And then there are your own personal preferences. You'd be surprised how much of English grammar, vocabulary and punctuation is actually just plain old personal choice . . . or a clean fit for your genre.

4. If you're writing a fiction book set in a world other than the one we live in, give me a little vocabulary list if you know your language will get exotic. That way . . . I won't question every non-word you use. (I share my "wolrd's" character vocabulary spreadsheet in the same folder in Dropbox that I have the Scrivener file that my editor's working on.)

5. Give me an upfront word count. I'll have a much better idea of turnaround time if you're flexible on that, and I can give you a more accurate quote. The quote I give you depends on the length, the extent of editing the document calls for, and your requested turnaround.

6. Directly related to that—please tell me your required turnaround time. If you want it tomorrow, let me know and I'll do everything in my power to make that happen, depending on your length. If it needs to be fast, you'll get it fast; it'll cost more, but you'll get it. If you can wait longer, that's great too. I'll work around everything else to get your document to you on time, as long as I know your deadline.

7. That little sample I do for every new client has another important purpose: I get to see what kind of editing you need. You may only need copyediting or proofreading on your draft, or it may call for a substantive job. It depends on the work I see on this document.

If you produce many different types of documents— maybe a mixture of several genres of fiction and non-fiction—so that your work comes to me radically different each time, **I may ask you for a (shorter) sample more frequently.** Maybe not every time, but your next document could call for entirely different editing.

Once We Hand Our Draft off to Our Editor

Here's the procedure our editors follow.

1. Make sure the entire draft is there, or the portion of the draft the writer has indicated was sent.

2. If it's on software that requires saving, such as Word, make sure an "edit" version of the doc is saved.

(If it's on Scrivener, the first thing I'll do is make sure all docs are open in the binder. Also in Scrivener, there's no need for constant saving as in Word. Indeed, do *not* save if you received the doc in Dropbox. It'll save itself.)

3. Read through the entire draft in Scrivener's Editor pane, section by section, chapter by chapter. This read-through gets no edits; its purpose is to acclimate myself to the content and see what patterns come up.

4. Go back to the beginning and start reading again, this time for editing. This process will be much slower than the initial read-through.

5. Watch out for patterns—capitalizations or lack of, special spellings, unusual punctuation.

6. Check for accuracy in the information given.

7. Watch out for smoothness and flow in the writing.

8. Catchy words or phrases: If there are none provided, see if I can suggest one or two—providing they add to the information given and the flow of the prose.

9. When finished editing each chapter or section, I go through the document again from the beginning, looking for anything left out, and then I make the needed changes.

10. Remember to keep saving if your program requires it.

Our Editor's Part in Scrivener

- As our editors make changes, they use Scrivener's "Label" function to color-mark each chapter "Editor Edits" as they go. This is to keep track of their progress. (Video Tutorial in bonuses)

- They change, highlight, comment, strikethrough, make notes and ask questions right inside Scrivener.

- Once our editor is completely finished with their edit, they make sure all of the files in our novel are marked "Editor Edits" and they close out of the file and don't touch it again. (I've gone so far as to remove their sharing privileges from Dropbox, just in case. Or I simply move the file out of the shared folder.)

Now that we've got our draft back from our editor, let's go take a look.

DAY 9: FINALIZATION

WISK

"You said you were editing it! That's what I did. It looks like you gut shot my novel! Oh, those are just flesh wounds."

Don't Panic.

When you get your very first draft back from an editor, you're going to freak out. There will be red lines and comments, and "suggestions" everywhere. And your little author ego is going to wonder what the hell just happened.

Because though you are so close to your story that everything seems obvious, from the outside, there will be . . . questions. "Why did your hero do this here? He's clearly too scared to do that." Or, "What do you mean by this word, because that is not what that word means." And what I got called out on in this book, even after I harped about contractions. "You need to use more contractions.

This is too formal."

You *will* have a high school English class flashback to Mrs. Backlund, drilling Shakespeare's "Out, out brief candle. Life's but a walking shadow. A poor player that struts—" OMG, Mrs. Backlund got me!

Finalizing

After we get our file back from the editor, these are the steps we take to finalize it.

- Move the Scrivener file out of the Dropbox shared folder and into a private one.

- Open the Scrivener project file and scroll the entire binder (the outline on the left), making sure everything looks "clean" and there are no documents missing.

- The next thing we do is snapshot that entire outline (our novel's top-level folder, chapter folders and documents) in the binder again, so we can compare the editor's changes to the original snapshot we made just before we sent it to them.

- Then we proceed folder by folder, chapter by chapter through every document in the file, "accepting" changes, reviewing our editor's comments and cleaning up things we might have missed.

- At the end of that, we run the spelling and grammar checker one last time (you never know).

- After that, as a final check, I like to compile the final draft into a .pdf file and shuttle through the pages, skimming to make sure that blank spaces, missing pages, or weird dangling one-sentence pages didn't happen.

- I check the front matter and back matter for my novels as well. (People do read them.)

- After that, I snapshot the entire directory tree in the Scrivener binder again, so I have a final version.

- If you're like me, you might skim-read through the entire thing again just to make certain you got everything.

Bravo! Pop champagne!

Get ready for self-publishing!

The Extra Mile

Even after we compile our drafts inside Scrivener into .mobi files for Kindle or .pdf files for CreateSpace, there's a bit more "editing"—sanity checking—that can be done.

Check your interior files locally.

Open your novel's compiled contents in a .pdf previewer or in the downloadable Kindle application, as the case may be, and make sure everything looks correct. Pay attention to the links and the Table of Contents. Check each one to make sure they go where they're supposed to.

Upload and check them again.

After you upload your files to self-publish on those platforms, each of them has an online book previewer. Use it.

It will check for things like spelling errors, text outside the printable margins and other things that you can't see until the final version is uploaded.

I always use the online Kindle and CreateSpace preview-er applications as one last sanity check, and have found things that were missed by human eyes each time.

You can go so far as to order a print copy from Create-Space to proofread a physical version. Kindle has a downloadable previewer application that you can use to see how your novel will look on several different book readers.

Published is better than perfect.

All this approaches trying to get your draft to borderline "perfect," but perfect isn't published. At a certain point you have to let it go and click "publish."

No matter how much you do, someone will find *something* wrong and let you know in a review—it's inevitable. But there's only so much you *can* do.

Congratulations! Your novel is officially . . . edited.

FICTION WRITING BASICS

PRE-EDITING

Before you write

That wasn't so bad, but we could've made all that editing even easier.

In this second section, I'll go over the very basics of writing and punctuating fiction dialogue.

Not only did we have to learn what and where we needed to put all that fancy prose and all that ferocious dialogue you penned in *Nine Day Novel: Writing*, but, from a writer's perspective, we really should've been editing as we went.

But Steve, you said *specifically,* "*Don't* edit as you write." Do you mean to tell me that now, that was all just a bunch of. . .? You've got to be kidding me!

Let me explain.

The Second Half of This Book

If you're like me, and you love to refresh your memory

and practice often, then the second half of this book is about helping you **understand or review the basics of fiction dialogue, exposition, sentence structure and action beats.** It'll help you make fewer mistakes as you write and then editing will take less time.

Examples

I find that I, and others I've helped figure this stuff out, learn best through examples that we can emulate. So, the following may seem a little redundant at times as we follow "Jim" and "Sally" through their "kitchen door-shutting dilemma," but the examples are the basis for punctuating fiction dialogue.

Here's What You Can Expect in This Section

Each chapter gives you basic examples of fiction dialogue sentences, action beats and exposition. This isn't story and style, this is writing fiction sentences for beginners.

I'll *begin* with the simplest dialogue and get progressively more sophisticated and useful as we go. I'll show you the "tricks" I wish I'd known before I started writing fiction.

QUICK TIP:

You see in that paragraph above where I wrote "tricks"? That's a quick tip to learn.

"Inconceivable!"

"You keep using that word, I do not think it means what you think it means." - Inigo Montoya, *The Princess Bride*

Bunny ears

You want to write something that *doesn't* mean what someone is saying, or that doesn't mean what the definition of the word is supposed to? Then "bunny-ear" with the first two fingers of both your hands, and put quotes around it.

When I say "tricks," it's because I mean there *are* no tricks.

Emphasize a Word.

If you want to *emphasize* one of your character's words in a line of dialogue, use italics to do that.

"What the *hell* are you talking about, Steve?"

Please do not say this: "What the HELL are you talking

about, Steve?" That is *not* how it's done. (Did I just utter an absolute? Noooo. . . Darth save me, I created a rule.)

Regardless, when my wife and I tell our kids we're having "private time," it means something else *entirely*.

Writing has "Rules"

There are a few things in fiction writing that remain pretty standard. But keep in mind that those "rules" are broken all the time.

This isn't high school English class, this is fiction storytelling. We want to drive story, plot and excitement for our reader. To do that we need to keep out of their way as they read—don't interrupt their brain with punctuation as they get immersed in the story.

Your goal—keep your reader reading.

Sometimes "correct"—strict adherence to style rules—messes with the reader's ability to follow the story. Your main goal is to keep them reading, so we're going to review some ways to stay out of our reader's way.

Staying Consistent

Above all, the standard you need to hold yourself to in this section is. . .

Stay consistent

When you're rich and famous, your publisher will have one of their editors clean up your "mess." Until then, you're going to do what works, do what other fiction writers do and most of all, *stay consistent.*

It's easy to clean up something that's written consistently "wrong," in someone else's opinion, but very difficult to clean up a draft that's wrong or right only part of the time.

Example:
STEG is my permafree prequel novella, introducing my readers to *The Fallen* series of dark fantasy thrillers.

It's the irreverent story of the Garden of Eden from Lucifer's perspective, before he was cast down to the pit. In it, the angels speak very formally.

While writing that novella for three days and then switching up to write this book, I'd stopped using contractions so purposefully that this book didn't have the informal "friendly" tone it should've.

My editor actually pointed this out to me in her comments several times before I vowed to go back through the draft and fix it.

But, by staying consistent, I was able to go back and find all the common contractions—like he's, it's and you're—and fix them pretty quickly.

QUICK TIP:
I have a cheat sheet. It's an Excel spreadsheet with all the vocabulary from the world of my fiction series, how made-up things are spelled, and what words characters say the wrong way—things like that. I do all of that so I can stay consistent across each novel in the 10-book series.

Example:
I used the term "warmark" for the emblem that angel wings make when they're pressed tightly against an angel's back. It's like a shield or a banner in medieval times of whose army you belong to.

The issue was, no one agreed on how to spell it. Internet, dictionaries, me, my editor. . . "Warmark" or "war mark" or "war-mark." So we had to pick one and stick with it. The trouble was, I kept forgetting which one we chose.

In every novel, I had to go to the spreadsheet and double-check how we decided to spell it. And each time I had to do a global-find-replace and clean it up.

DIALOGUE BASICS

WISK

"I like a little 'how' in my how-to guides. I guess I'm kinda funny that way."

In *NDN: Writing*, we talked about what to write, where to put it in your story, and some hardcore ways that I write novels quickly. Now, let's talk a little more about that thing I believe most how-to books leave out—the actual "how."

Here's What You'll learn

Learn to write sentences.

Fiction sentences, not those high school subject-predicate-object monsters.

A riddle? Sort of. Here's what I mean:

All the sentence structure you learned in your entire life can be boiled down to some basic rules that relate to sentence building for fiction. Most fiction author advice starts off as "show, don't tell."

That's fabulous! But you'd probably ask what I did. *How do I do that?* And I don't want you to "show" me a line from *The Great Gatsby*, hoping that I will just "get" it. Because I won't. *Tell* me—break it down for me.

The three basics

You need to know these three basic things to physically write fiction. Notice I didn't say "tell a compelling story."

1 - Exposition

The insertion of important background or scene and setting information within a story—narrative that *tells* the reader something you want them to know.

In novels, exposition is delivered as a character—many times the main character in the book—talking and telling you about the world they live in. Or, commonly also, as an omniscient voice setting the scene, time, place and mood before you dive into the action.

2 - Action Beats

Your characters, doing something physical, and other characters reacting to it. Or events taking place around your characters.

3 - Dialogue

Your characters talking to each other or thinking in their own head.

Learn the basics, then get "fancy."

Everything in fiction writing gets more complicated as writers get better. We like to show off our command of the skills, right?

The problem is that it can get very difficult to make things simple.

As adults, I think we purposefully make things more complicated, believing that we're making them better. But the basics of storytelling are found . . . well, in the basics.

QUICK TIP:

Go read a children's fiction book. Like fourth or fifth grade level. It's clear what's going on, the words are easy to read, the punctuation and grammar are easy to under-stand, and the characters and plot are easy to follow. In short, the author knows their audience and writes to them in their language, their style and with clearly-defined dialogue tags and sentence structure.

Fiction Storytelling

(Funny, they don't call it story *showing.)*

Use a mix of exposition, dialogue and action beats to weave a tale about characters being challenged, growing and then overcoming. That's done in a million different writers' "voices."

You'll find your voice—your style—but the basic structure and mechanics won't change. Only how you apply them in your story will vary.

If you want to learn the pace and structure needed to tell a story, in *NDN: Writing* I cover the Four Part Story Struc-ture in lightsaber-slashing, gory detail.

Exposition example:

A long time ago, in a world not unlike your own, a small group of people decided whose novels would be published, how they would be published, and how much money authors would make from their books. But that was a long time ago. Today, things are different.

Simply put, *that* is exposition—telling the reader something. Doing that as direct information to your reader, whether using a main character or an omniscient voice, is exposition story-*telling*.

Dialogue Example:

Story-*showing* your reader what is happening. Let your characters speak.

"I got rejected again," Jim told Sally.

"You know," Sally said, "that's big-house publishing for ya. Almost dead, if you ask me. Killing you for sure. Why don't you self-publish?"

"That's pretty bleak," Jim said, "don't you think? Anyway, I don't know how to do that."

Sally laughed. "I'll show you," she said.

Now that's some pretty basic and boring "he said-she said" dialogue, but it's the basis for all fiction character interaction. And in that is the key to writing faster and spending less time editing at the end.

QUICK TIP:
Fiction paragraphs are most often structured with an indented first line and no spaces between paragraphs. Non-fiction has no indented first line and a space between paragraphs.

We typically use Adobe Garamond Pro font at 11-12pt for fiction, and Helvetica 14pt for non-fiction books.

Basic Dialogue Structure

Dialogue tags

A dialogue tag is a descriptive word plus the character saying it. "He said," "she said" and "they said" are dialogue tags. The most common dialogue tags? Said, says, say—depending on tense.

Examples of other dialogue tags:

- he scoffed
- she whispered
- Sally spoke softly
- Life screeched (When I wrote *The Fallen* series, the angels had many bird-like qualities. One of them is that they screech like a hawk when they shout or scream, thus a custom dialogue tag was created and further immerses the reader in that world. Yes, you can do that.)

Everything is negotiable.

Some authors have stopped using "asked" in dialogue questions, preferring to let the reader's already-conditioned eyes skip right over the word "said" as they are so used to seeing it. They replace "asked" with "he or she said."

In fact, many of them stick to the dialogue tag "said" to let their dialogue, situation and character reactions define the intensity of the dialogue.

Example:

"Can you get the door?" Jim said.

Perfectly fine, and in the middle of a bunch of dialogue no one even notices it.

Common ways to structure dialogue sentences

- "The car's parked in the driveway. I think it's finally cooled down," Sally said.
- "The car's parked in the driveway. I think it's finally cooled down," said Sally.
- "The car's parked in the driveway," Sally said. "I think it's finally cooled down."
- "The car's parked in the driveway," said Sally. "I think it's finally cooled down."
- Sally said, "The car's parked in the driveway. I think it's finally cooled down."
- "The car's parked in the driveway." Sally sighed. "I think it's finally cooled down."

I show you those, because they make up the bulk of character exchanges using fiction sentence structure.

Yes, everything gets more complicated and prettier as we get better. As we progress, we weave in exposition, action beats, and pauses and interruptions, and our own author "voice."

But we start by knowing the basics—how to hold your sword if we were sword-fighting—before we get comfortable stringing them all together in the large opera battle called writing a novel.

Super Simple Dialogue

Structurally, the comma goes after the dialogue tag if it comes before the dialogue. It goes inside the quotes if the dialogue tag follows it.

> Jim said, "Shut the door, please."
> "Okay," replied Sally.

Now that we've constructed the dialogue sentences correctly, what does this sentence *show* the reader? Well, for starters, who's doing the talking—critical knowledge for a reader. Then it conveys some information.

The door's open, Jim doesn't like it or just doesn't want it that way. He's not afraid to tell someone else to shut it rather than do it himself. But he *is* willing to at least be semi-polite about it.

And Sally? Well, Sally just complies with his request and offers no disagreement or resistance. This tells the reader nothing, but maybe . . . a lot.

Maybe Jim's cold or the wind's blowing or maybe they're both cold. The reader's free to interpret and project themselves into the scene. And that's what you want. Which is why the "experts" say show, don't tell.

QUICK TIP:
The rules are more guidelines than anything else.

Many stories, including huge *Star Wars*-style sagas and epic novels, start off with long expositional narrative to set the scene, time and setting for the reader or viewer.

Star Wars just runs it as a credit roll on the screen for you to read before the movie starts! Now *that's* beating you over the head with exposition! But it works, so don't be afraid to break the rule of show don't tell.

Action Beats

Let's give the reader a little more to chew on.

> Jim shivered. "Shut the door, please," he said.
> Sally was closer to the blown-open door than Jim, so she reached over and shut it. "Okay," she replied.

It's a little clearer what's going on here. The action beat

at the beginning of Jim's sentence and the exposition and action beat leading into the dialogue in Sally's sentence makes that possible.

Jim's cold, he wants the door shut. Sally's closer and better positioned to shut it quickly to stop the wind from coming in. Jim and Sally have some kind of relationship. We don't really know what it is, but it's there in between the lines. Still, Sally's willing to do what Jim asks and Jim feels free to ask it . . . politely.

Replacing a dialogue tag with an action beat

Dialogue tags are meant to keep the reader informed of who's talking—which character is speaking and to whom, or themselves. So, though technically correct, the dialogue tags at the end of those sentences are a bit redundant, given that we already established who was about to speak by giving them an action beat.

So, this example might work better and is less cluttered. Remember—opinion, style and developing your own voice.

Jim shivered. "Shut the door, please."

Standing closer to the blown-open door than he was, Sally reached over and slammed it. "Okay."

Less cluttered and still totally clear to the reader who said what to whom and when even without dialogue tags. But wait! You changed a word, Steve. Yes, I did, didn't I?

Sally "slammed" the door this time.

So we cleaned up the dialogue—put some action beats instead of dialogue tags. And we only changed one word, which changed the entire "feel" of this exchange.

Sally slammed the door in response to Jim's request . . . or was the wind blowing so hard she had to? We leave the white space for the reader to project their own thoughts.

But we could have done it better. . .

Jim shivered. "Shut the door, please."
Sally reached over and slammed it. "Okay."

There really wasn't a reason to beat the reader over the head with the exposition in front of Sally's action beat. The fact that she "reached over" is plenty to show the reader that she was most likely closer to the door than Jim.

QUICK TIP:

When you first start out, you'll be tempted to make sure that the reader knows *exactly* what you're trying to convey. But readers are smart—they figure things out with minimal shoving and pushing from you. A sentence like. . .

"I most certainly will not shut the door, Jim," Sally said indignantly.

. . .borders on bludgeoning your reader with redundant information. The way your character speaks should make it clear without hammering adverbs like "indignantly."

Basic Structures You Should Learn . . . *then* Break

Examples:

Dialogue tag up front

Jim said, "Shut the door, please."

Comma before the quote to separate dialogue tag after the dialogue

"Shut the door," said Jim.

A question

"Can you shut the door, please?" asked Jim.

Note that "asked" is not capitalized because it's a dialogue tag. It doesn't matter that the "?" ends the dialogue sentence before it.

As a side note, Scrivener's grammar checker always wants me to put a "?" where that period at the end is. Totally incorrect.

Exclamation

"Shut the door . . . please!" shouted Jim.

Once again, just like with the question mark, "shouted" is not capitalized, because it's a dialogue tag.

Exposition and action beat lead in

Jim always intended to fix his rickety kitchen door, but "distractions" had kept him from it. He sighed, closed his eyes and shook his head slowly. "Shut the door, please," he said.

Sally just stared at him. He had that "look" on his face again. She knew all about what that meant. She raised her eyebrows back at him—it had been a week. "Okay," she said, smiling in front of her. She slammed the door shut.

QUICK TIP:

When you have only two characters present and they're having a conversation back and forth, it's **perfectly acceptable to omit some dialogue tags** as long as the reader won't be confused as to who's speaking.

"Could you shut the door?" Jim said. He winced and stared at the frying eggs. "Please?"

Sally got up and walked across the old farmhouse kitchen. "Okay," she said, shutting the door.

"Thank you."

It's crystal clear that Jim's the one who said "thank you" so there's no need to bang the reader over the head with a dialogue tag.

I'll leave it to the reader to determine if Sally and Jim were communicating about taking out the trash or . . . something else.

And that's the beauty of storytelling—until you're ready to hit your reader over the head with your plot points or story milestones, they should be free to move through your tale with their own prejudices and predispositions, unhindered by oppressive dialogue tags.

It's a Symphony

Your novel is a symphony of words and vocabulary and punctuation and grammar all led—"conducted"—in your own personal style. Your "voice."

When we get better—mixing in dialogue, well-placed dialogue tags and action beats—it's like directing a concerto, a musical opera revolving around our hero, highlighting his or her struggle and journey.

We strive to create an image in our reader's mind. One that'll transport him or her out of their boring world and into our exciting one.

Making subtle changes in positioning and strategically omitting some information, we allow the reader to project themselves into our story. We can completely change the feel of an exchange, a scene, a chapter, and an entire novel.

It's why no two writers can write the same, and why a story can be told over and over again by different authors and still be entertaining and exciting.

Semi-pertinent trivia segue

A story, because I'm a storyteller and this subject is starting to bore the hell out of you, right?

My family and I love the TV series *Once Upon a Time*. The writers have done such a fantastic job of reworking and intertwining the age-old Disney stories that it's simply amazing.

On our way back from a trip to Whistler in BC Canada, we were looking up attractions that we could visit in Vancouver, and lo and behold OUAT is filmed in Steveston, BC Canada! (Just south of Vancouver.)

Forget that it's where OUAT is filmed—the town's named "Steveston," for crying out loud! That's karma!

One-hour detour later, and we were standing where Mr. Gold (Rumpelstiltskin) hatches all of his evil plots. Amazing!

Gratuitous story? I have a method to my madness.

If you can write a story, craft a tale, spin a yarn that is so enthralling to your readers/fans that they will drive two hours out of their way to see one of the locations in it. . . On that day, you'll have approached mastering your chosen craft.

You aren't a master!

What are you talking about, Steve, *you* aren't a master?

True enough, young Jedi, [pulls lightsaber from sheath and fires up the red light] *VVVMMMM.* . . However, each day I revisit the basics of writing and strive to learn something new.

Everything from the worst FREE ebook to the best $0.99 value gem I've ever read has something to teach me. So I pull out my lightsaber (laptop and Scrivener) every day, and then I practice and learn.

More Writing to Edit

Put dialogue tags up front.

Many budding fiction authors—I went back and read my early stuff and I was *so* guilty of this—put dialogue tags too far into a sentence.

By the time the reader knows who's speaking, the speaking's over. That means the entire time they were reading, they may have had no clue who was talking until the end. That's not reader friendly. And in editing we would have to clean that up . . . unless we didn't do that in the first place.

Examples:

- Jim paced the floor in the kitchen. "Shut the door, please," he said behind him at Sally.
- Jim paced the kitchen floor. "Shut the door," he said behind him. "Please."
- "Shut the door," Jim said behind him. "Please."
- "Shut the door," Jim said, "please." (Also works.)
- Sally looked at Jim. He had that look. "Okay."
- "Okay," Sally said, slamming the door to the kitchen. Jim had that "look" again.
- Jim looked at Sally. "Shut the door, please," he said to her.
- "Okay."

QUICK TIP:
One of the best pieces of feedback I ever got on my novels was that my buddy editor, was getting lost, trying to figure out what scene, group of characters, or place in time she was reading.

It took Lise two or three sentences into the opening paragraph of the chapter.

I jump around a lot in my novels—back and forth from past to present—changing which group of characters the reader is following. So I went back through and read all of the opening sentences in my chapters and sure enough, it took a sentence or two to figure out who, where, what and when you were reading about.

I changed it so it was more clear right away what place in time and which characters you had jumped to.

Advanced Exposition and Dialogue

By combining exposition, action beats, and character dialogue, we learn to tell amazing, fantastic stories that stay out of our readers' way while informing them as they read. And we do all of that without letting them figure out that's what we're doing.

As far as a reader knows, they're in an action-packed story, racing with their hero to solve the mystery, defeat the bad guy and save the day. A great mix of techniques makes this possible while conveying mood, setting, scene, speech, action and backstory . . . all interwoven at the same time.

Say what?

Trust me, you get better at it. And that's why I harped on you to write, write, write!

Remember that conductor? Ever wonder what the first symphony that conductor ever led sounded like? I'll give you a hint—crap! And that's why he or she never got in front of a live audience until he or she did what? . . . Anyone?

This is yet another example of *practice* makes you better. Not perfect. Better.

Example:

The wind pelted the outside of Jim's little white farmhouse and the old wooden door to his kitchen flew open. He'd intended to fix the latch—so many times—but he had . . . "distractions." He turned his attention from frying eggs on his grandma's old iron stove and looked at Sally.

Sally, Jim's girlfriend turned ex and back again, sat sideways in her favorite rickety kitchen chair, drinking her morning coffee. She smiled—Jim knew just how she liked it. She fiddled with her frizzed and frazzled hair. And though Jim didn't know it, she'd grinned at his back the entire time he cooked. She barely noticed the door fly open—lost in the heat of last night.

Jim smiled over his shoulder. "Could ya get that?" Remembering Sally's preference for politeness, he winked at her and said, "Pretty please?"

Sally cocked her head a little. Maybe Jim could be "trained" after all. Living out on his farm, all alone after they. . . She closed her eyes and shook her head. *Leave it alone*, she thought. "Okay," she said. Then she got up and fought the wind to get to the wide-open door, now banging against the inside of the kitchen almost as loudly as the headboards had last night.

Jim's white dress shirt fit Sally about ten sizes too big. It flipped and flapped, snapping her on the backside as the wind whipped all the extra material. She knew Jim would be staring at the bottom of it, remembering.

The shirt made a great nightgown, but wasn't much against the wind and rain blasting through the kitchen door. By the time she slammed the door shut, the front of it was soaked and see-through.

Sally smiled as she turned around. It had been a week since her last visit—Jim wasn't above it—but there was something different this time. Something . . . better. She slipped back down into her chair just as Jim was putting her favorite breakfast onto her plate. She smiled up at him. *Maybe it will work this time.*

Jim tipped the still sizzling frying pan back and looked at Sally's plate, filled with her favorite over-easy eggs, peppered just enough. Then he glanced up. He could hardly stop himself from staring at her. . . He smiled and pretended to look her in the eyes. "What?" he said. But they both already knew.

That got me—hang on. [wipes tear]

So, that was roughly 300-400 words of a scene where I conveyed a ton of information. And if I did it right, you imagined Jim's farmhouse kitchen, and Sally in his shirt. I left it open for you to imagine what *he* was wearing. (Who knows, maybe Jim likes to cook naked.)

Regardless, you should *not* have been reading dialogue tags, action beats and punctuation. You should've just pictured yourself as Jim or Sally as the case may be, and what it would feel like to be in the kitchen making or being served breakfast after. . .

A Little Deeper Into Dialogue

If you noticed in that last example, there were some extra things I threw in. Let's talk about them.

The first one:

. . .he had . . . "distractions."

I used an ellipsis to add a little tension, maybe a pause for a little tongue-in-cheek humor, and then followed it up with a quoted word. I did that to show Jim's thoughts signifying that Sally isn't actually a distraction so much as she's something else entirely to him. Let the reader figure out exactly who Sally is to Jim as the story progresses.

"Sally, Jim's girlfriend turned ex and back again, sat sideways. . ."

QUICK TIP:
Even the master (We all know that's Stephen King, right?) admits that simply describing characters by their body traits—hair/eye color and physical features—borders on that boring "telling" sin we spoke of earlier.

So, and this is his suggestion, rather than doing it that way—describing body parts in gory detail, leaving nothing to the reader's imagination—leave the reader free to project what they want the character to look like in their mind.

Leave blanks for your reader to fill in. Give them a type of person or a half-description of someone and then let them imagine the rest of that person in any way they want.

Sally's description above

". . .girlfriend turned ex then back again. . ."

That puts a distinct picture in my mind of who Sally is, who she is to Jim, and it sets up a lot of the rest of the scene. This allows the reader to project a ton of their own feelings onto a character.

Still don't believe me?

J.K. Rowling's description of Hagrid in *Harry Potter* is a prime example. "He looked simply too big to be allowed."

That's leaving it to the imagination of the reader. Hagrid . . . is *huge*.

Back to fiction sentence structure. *Whoop-pshhh!*

Super Advanced Sentences

Em-dash

Named because it's the width of the typed letter "m," by the way.

Em-dashes have a lot of cool and functional uses. Let's look at some em-dash examples.

Explanation segue

The reason or explanation for the preceding statement or sentence.

"She barely noticed the door fly open—lost in the heat of last night."

Sideways segue

It's also okay to interrupt something to quickly slip in a little piece of information for the reader, and then ram them back into the action.

"It had been a week since her last visit—he wasn't above it—but there was something different this time."

And proving my point, my writing buddy Lise's notes after proofing this section were "I have no idea what you mean here." That was *exactly* the point.

Little segues in your characters' minds will serve to help you foreshadow—start a little mystery in your reader's mind that you'll solve later. This allows the reader's thoughts to run wild until you *want* to let them in on the secret.

Above what? What wasn't Jim above? I want to know!

We'll cover more on em-dashes later. Which leads me to. . .

Ellipsis example:

"Living out on his farm, all alone after they. . ."

That line above—some say you shouldn't, but every once in a while, I like to leave a little dangling mystery at the end of a paragraph. Something for the reader to figure out. Some unspoken or unfinished sentence that could be finished or interpreted many different ways.

After they what? . . . Broke up? . . . The town banished Jim? After *what* happened? It's an unfinished thought and sentence inside Sally's mind that begs the reader to try and figure it out.

Thought

And that brings me to thought inside a character's mind. The reader gets to "see" it.

"Maybe it will work this time."

Sally's thought to herself is italicized—not quoted. (It's confusing, because we *are* quoting from the above excerpts, so there are quotes around that example, but their purpose is to reference the speech above.

So this is a case where the "rules" get in the way.) **It should have no quotes when you write it.**

Maybe it will work this time.

Thought is punctuated with a dialogue tag as if it were spoken speech. And let me tell you, the first time I saw a thought as a question with a dialogue tag after it, I said "no way." Yes . . . *way.*

Will it work this time? she thought.

And even as I typed that, Scrivener tried to capitalize the "s" in "she" because it thinks that the sentence before it ended. Nope, that dialogue tag—"she thought"—is part of the entire sentence.

Some disagree on dialogue tags for thought. They argue that if you're just going to put a dialogue tag that says "she thought," why italicize the actual thought? But . . . I'm not always going to put a dialogue tag on thought. So we call it out as thought with a dialogue tag the first time we do it in a scene and then maybe after that we believe that the reader understands italics as thought and leave the tags out.

Summary

I'll wrap up our introduction to sentence structure and dialogue punctuation talk by saying there are all kinds of variations and ways to convey your story. These punctuations are some basic examples to use as building blocks.

A lot of these work for me, so I use them. Why? Because at the end of writing my first draft, I want as clean a draft as I can get to cut down on proofing time.

So I found some techniques and structures I like, I "own" them, I stay consistent using them, and I write a ton, practicing with them. If I find new ones I like and figure out how to use well, I add them.

Once my editor and I figure out how I write, and agree that it's okay to do it that way, I stick with it and she knows what to look for or what I mean when I use a particular punctuation.

For instance, I'm an em-dash freak. My editor knows that and adjusts accordingly, watching out for them, chopping them and reprimanding me when she has to.

DIALOGUE EXAMPLES

WISK

"Art is imitation? Well, I can do *that*."

I'm serious, someone famous said that. Yep, I butchered it. The original is actually better than mine and has a ton of meaning for indie authors.

"Art begins in imitation and ends in innovation." - Mason Cooley

Translation: Learn how other people do it until you get good, and then do what you want and let them follow you for a change.

Don't worry, if you're successful enough—you make a lot of money—they'll call you enlightened and ahead of your time. If you aren't successful—you don't sell well—they'll call you a hack.

Ahh, the life we have chosen!

But just what does a beautiful story/novel look like anyway? It's a bit like dating—one person's "perfect" is another's "pathetic."

Examples of Dialogue Sentences

First, a recap of the basic rules. . .

In dialogue, commas, question marks and periods all go in specific places.

When your characters speak, that goes inside the quotation marks. Dialogue tags and action beats are outside the quotations.

Dialogue sentences start with a capital.

"Get the door," Jim said.

Sometimes there is no dialogue tag, like when the character is known or implied by the context.

"Get the door, please."

Or a dialogue tag at the end

"Get the door," Jim said.

(Notice the comma, Jim's name is capped and the period

is at the end of the sentence.)

Or the reverse, in which case the word "said" is not capitalized.

"Get the door," said Jim.

Dialogue tag up front

Jim said, "Get the door."

Putting an action beat with the dialogue sentence. The action beat at the end tells something, but is inside the same sentence.

"Get the door," Jim said, not wanting to get it himself.

Action beat and dialogue tag up front and question at the end.

Continuing to fry the eggs, Jim asked, "Could you get the door?"

Dialogue tag splitting the sentence is okay too and lets you insert a pause in speech without special characters. There's no capitalization on the second half, because this is the same sentence. And the dialogue tag has commas on both sides.

"Hey," Jim said, "could you get the door . . . please?"

Throw in an **action beat in the middle**.

"Close the door," Jim said, stirring the eggs, then he finished it the way he knew Sally wanted him to, "please?" (Though this one is a bit awkward.)

Split two sentences with dialogue tags.

"Close the door," Jim said, realizing right away it was a mistake. "Please."

Questions and exclamations

The door to Jim's kitchen flung open and the rain rushed in. "Close the damn door!"
Sally frowned at him and closed the door.

Dialogue tag and action beat at the end

"Could you close the door?" Jim asked, casually stirring the eggs.

"Close the damn door!" Jim said to Sally, annoyed that it had taken her so long to get up.

Interrupting a character's speech

Here's where things get tricky . . . and more useful. We can interrupt a character's speech by giving them something to do in the middle of it with an action beat. Took me a while to get used to seeing it. Now, I love it.

Put in a little action as people speak. Because real people do things while they talk.

"Could you"—Jim stirred the eggs more quickly—"close the door? I can't get to it right now."

Or an indirect thought in the middle

"Close the door"—Jim thought they might have time for one more—"I've got an . . . idea."

There's no dialogue tag when a character interrupts his/her own speech. No spaces, no commas, no capitals—nothing. And the action is set off by em-dashes.

You can do the same thing with indirect dialogue. No quotes required for indirect dialogue.

Jim asked Sally to close the door—*it wouldn't be good*—because he didn't want Jennifer to show up and see them.

Quoted Speech

If one of your characters is relating something that someone *else* said, that will be inside the primary dialogue quotations.

English quotation variations

In the U.S., as you've been seeing here, primary dialogue takes double quotations. Within them, quoted speech gets single quotations.

In British English, dialogue gets single quotes with double quotes within. Canadian English generally follows the American model, although not always. Australia and New Zealand use the British style. We'll continue here in American English.

American-Canadian:

"I heard *you* said, 'Jim's a jerk.' "

British, Australian, New Zealand:

'I heard you said, "Jim's a jerk." '

If your quoted dialogue butts up against your primary-dialogue, double quotation marks, you have to put a space or it looks very weird. Unreadable weird. Take a look:

"Jennifer said that you said, 'Jim's a jerk.' " (Single quote + space + double quote)

It just freaks me out. So I try not to end that quoted speech at the end of the dialogue.

"Jennifer heard you say, 'Jim's a jerk.' Is that true?"

Now that's a lot of dialogue structure to take in, but you have to think of all these as tools you can use to break up that "he said-she said" dialogue that gets boring and monotonous.

But I'm with ya—I might need a Piña Colada to keep going. Be right back. Hang on. Mmmm. . .

Okay, let's go.

Deeper Into the Em-dash

You remember this one, right?

Dialogue cutoff

Dialogue can be interrupted wherever it makes sense. Usually **if a character abruptly stops him or herself, the cutoff is at the end of the word**. (You rarely stop yourself mid-word.)

If another character cuts them off, then break the word on a syllable, or at least at the point where the reader may still be able to figure out what word that character was going to say.

Interrupt a word in a logical place.

"Close the damn d—"
Sally slammed the kitchen door before the word even came out of Jim's mouth. Ordering her around? Not happening!

Now, even crazier: If Sally is really annoyed and anticipated Jim giving her yet another order in their on-again, off-again relationship, she might do this:

Jim frowned. "Could y—"

"I'm getting to it!" Sally shouted, slamming the door.

"—close the door," Jim muttered to himself, wondering if last night was a mistake.

(My Scrivener autocorrect wanted to make that "c" in "close the door" a capital "C," but it's not. It's a continuation of the sentence Jim started, but got interrupted before he could finish.)

A loud noise interrupting thought

Jim stopped stirring the eggs and thought, *did we really just do th*

—

CRASH! The kitchen door flung open and slammed into the wall. The wind howled through it like he and Sally had last night.

Em-dashes have other uses.

Like you saw before, the quick segue.

If something happens or a character has a quick thought in the middle of a complete thought, action, or sentence, then it can be set off as a quick sideways segue with em-dashes.

Jim kept stirring the eggs—*she likes 'em just so*—and Sally stared at his bare back.

Switching directions in thought or speech

Jim frowned down at the frying pan. "That door's always—close it for me, will ya?"

Ellipses

If you have a character that frequently forgets what they were going to say, doesn't finish sentences or just gets distracted, you use an ellipsis to show their speech trailing off while they search their mind for the. . . Wait, I forgot what I was gonna. . . Oh, yeah, the right word.

Daydreaming

"Can you get the. . ." Jim's mind filled with flashes from the previous night. He smiled. "Close the door, would ya please?"

A pause in speech or thought

Jim said, "Could you get the door . . . please?"

Jim raged down at the frying eggs. I wish she would just . . . get the damn door, he thought.

Or an unfinished sentence

"I'm sorry, your eggs are. . ." Jim said, hesitating to tell Sally that he had burned them . . . again.

Or trailing off at the end

"I'm sorry," Jim said, "but your eggs got. . ."

My favorite—the unfinished question

This leaves the reader open to insert anything they think your character might have been asking.

"Hey, Sally," Jim said, glancing at the stairs to the second floor of the farmhouse, "you think we should go and. . .?"

Jim's a naughty man. Or maybe he wants Sally to help him vacuum. You don't know. Don't judge me!

Using Names in Dialogue

Hey, I slipped something in on you up there. When Jim

was directly addressing Sally.

If one character speaks directly to another—addressing them by proper name or improper doesn't matter—you use a comma to separate the name from the rest of the dialogue. Here's what I mean.

"Close the door, Sally."

"Sally, could you close the door?"

Or if Jim has a pet name for Sally.

"Close the door, sugar."

My all-time favorite that still doesn't look right to me:

"Hey, Sally, could you close the door, please?"

Multiple Lines of Dialogue

Okay, now, here it comes. For all the windbags, blow-hard characters and monologuing villains you've written into your novel. . . (All villains monologue before they're about to deliver the death blow to the hero. It's their undoing, but they do it.)

Some of them, like Bain in *Batman*, do it while they're kicking the hero's ass in part three of the Four Part Story Structure—fight back and fail.

So if you write a blow-hard, bragger, Bain in *Batman*, or any other long-winded character, this section's for you . . . and them. Remember what I said about putting the character dialogue tags early in the sentence? Same goes for diatribe-prone people. Up front, let the reader know who's speaking, and then let the character speak.

Examples:

"Sally," Jim said, "I just want you to know. . . Well, last night was just one of those things. And I don't know if we should really start this up again. You know what happened last time. I don't think either of us wants the police here again, do we?"

or. . .

"Sally, I just want you to know," Jim said, pausing and wondering if he should wait until after. "Well, last night was just one of those things. And I don't know if we should really light this up or not. You know what happened last time. I don't think either of us wants the police here again, do we?"

Several paragraphs of dialogue together

This next one still doesn't look right to me, and Scrivener will yell at you every time you do it, saying you've forgotten to close a section of dialogue with an ending quotation mark. But . . . I've checked and my editor said, "That's the way it's done."

Only the last paragraph in a character's run-on dialogue gets ending quotations. Each paragraph gets its own open quotation and no closing quotation until the very last one.

I know—confusing, right? Only way I learn these things is through example.

Example:

"Sally, I just want you to know," Jim said, pausing and wondering if he really should say it to her now or wait until after. "Well, last night was just one of those things. And I don't know if we should really light this up or not. You know what happened last time. I don't think either of us wants the police here again, do we?

"What I'm trying to. . . You know what that got us last time—jail and a bunch of explaining to do at church the next day. I don't think either of us wants that. Not again."

Conspicuously missing closing quote on the first paragraph of dialogue. And in the next paragraph, we open up another quote and Jim keeps speaking.

No closing dialogue quote until the end of the last paragraph.

Switching Characters in Dialogue

You've already seen this, but it bears repeating: Each time the character changes, start a new paragraph.

"Close the door, please," said Jim.
"Okay," Sally replied.

I mean, how hard is that? It gets more complicated when you have other characters thinking about the character who's about to speak and/or exposition that refers to both characters right before one of them speaks, but let's take baby steps.

Time for some fun, because sentence structure is *killing* me.

ONOMATOPOEIA - BAM!

WISK

"Steve, I'm bored. *BAM!* Are you bored now?"

Steve, this is so boring. Sentence structure and dialogue punctuation? Come on, I'm a storyteller, not an English teacher.

Partially true. In reality, you're an author. More specifically, an independent author who needs to settle in for the long haul and conserve your energy (money) until you succeed. To do that, you'll need to cultivate many skills. One of them is learning sentence structure so you can write cleaner and edit faster.

But Darth, I just can't take any. . .

The sound of their voices trail off in my mind and I consider pulling out my lightsaber. *Can't use the stick all the time*, I think. *They'll get numb to it eventually. Carrot maybe?*

"Okay," I say, "we'll do something fun." The relief on their faces tells me it's the right decision.

Onomatopoeia — written sound

Sound like an old *Batman* episode? Where trumpets blast and then they flash the word *"BIFF!"* in front of a cheesy image of a star exploding around the word? Yes. Exactly!

In *FURY*, my novel about an angry young angel who resurrects back to life in order to redeem herself and get from Hell to Heaven. . . Fury wants something else, but I won't spoil it. Anyway, she ends up locked in a Mexican prison cell with her friends in Cancun, being tortured by some nasty bad guys.

Sue me, but I like visceral, violent action in my novels. Sometimes in order to put people in a concrete cell, strapped to a chair with your hero — have them "feel" like they are there — you want to show them sounds. Sounds like your poor teenage hero girl getting the crap kicked out of her in prison.

SMACK!

Fury's face lit up with fire as the big guard hit her again.

That's a very visceral word to me, and it makes me feel a certain way. Relating that feeling by saying, "He smacked her across the face," doesn't do it justice.

QUICK TIP:

In researching this part, I found one of the coolest websites ever. You can look up all manner of onomatopoeia—written sound. It's actually called—wait for it. . .

Written Sound

So fun and so cool.

Someone interrupted by a loud noise

Jim said, "Would you get the—"
SLAM! Sally swung the door closed as hard as she could.

The sound is actually good because it's another show don't tell example. I like that better than:

Jim said, "Would you get the—"

The sound of the kitchen door slamming shut startled Jim. Sally had slammed it as hard as she could.

Boring. . .

THE WRETCHED WRETCH RETCHED

WISK

"I don't know nothin' 'bout no grammarization and spel-lerizin' and vocabulistics, but I do know this . . . using proper English to write a fictional tale about guttural and greedy individuals rarely conveys to the reader the infor-mation that you intended to in the first place."

Lest you think that "vocabulistics" is a word that I made up for effect. . . Well, it is made up—*Guardians of the Galaxy*, Rocket the Raccoon, talking about Groot. (Hey, I got kids. Anyway, as old as I am, that movie's soundtrack rocked!)

And Darth Vader energized his lightsaber—he could see that they had had enough of the sidebars and segues. It was time for pain.

Grammar, Spelling, Vocabulary

Yes, back to the boring. I actually like vocabulary, be-cause it allows me to put a certain poetry in my prose. "Poison" in my pen, if you will.

So, get comfortable with the fact that one of the easiest things you can do to clean up your story, is using the spell-checker and the correct word for what you intend to say. Seemingly simple, yet ignored all the time.

This goes beyond knowing the difference between being a "loser" and a "looser." Believe me, the person who called me a "looser" in a review still invokes a snicker out of me.

QUICK TIP:
I couldn't remember the difference between invoke and evoke, so . . . I Googled it. And yes, Google is your friend while you're writing and afterward. Here's a definitive resource for understanding the difference between commonly confused words. I actually use this guy's website all the time to understand the difference between similar but often confused words.

Common Errors in English Usage

Before we go any farther . . . or is it further? Those always confused me. However, "farther" is distance and "further" is metaphorical, or figurative, distance. Farther has "far" in it. That's how you remember it. Where was I?

Oh yes, the title of this chapter.

"The Wretched Wretch Retched"

Wretched—in a very unhappy or unfortunate state (adjective)
Wretch—an unfortunate or unhappy person (noun)
Retched—vomited (verb)

I point this out because English is one of the most confusing languages to learn for a non-native speaker. So many words mean different things and are spelled differently, yet sound the exact same way.

Here's a couple of lists of the most commonly misused and often confused words in the English language. Be aware of them as you write:

100 most commonly confused words
100 most commonly misused words

My all-time nemesis favorite is "their, there, they're." When I'm writing over 1,000 words an hour, I interchange them all the time. That's why I add them to my proofing checklist. But you want to cut down on mistakes, right? These get easier to remember once you use them enough:

Their—possessive belonging to "them"
There—a physical place

They're—They are . . . as in "they are" going to the movies.

Oh, Darth, I just can't take much more of this dry, boring —

Me either! Let's get outta here!

CONTRACTIONS

WISK

"Those look painful. What are they? . . . Contractions. *What?* . . . Not *those* kind."

I was going to list them here, but it seemed gratuitously wasteful, so here's a list of the most common contractions:

List of Common English Contractions

Contractions in Dialogue

To speed up your dialogue and make it sound more authentic, you'll definitely want to use contractions. Spelling out "didn't" as "did not" seems too formal to readers, even when they're reading exposition. So, your characters get to use contractions, your action beats get to use them and even your narrator's expositional voice can use them.

That way, when one of your characters doesn't use a contraction, it's that much more powerful.

Jim howled down at the eggs in the frying pan.

Sally giggled at him. "I did *not* sound like that."

Eliminating a character

When you eliminate a character that pronounces part of a word, it gets an apostrophe (closing single quote) where the eliminated part would've been.

Do you think Jim and Sally were **playin'**, **stayin'** or **prayin'** last night?

Or at the front

'bout now—about now, as opposed to a boxing match
'cause—because as opposed to the reason for something
'course—of course

'Bout now, Steve, I don't know what to think. 'Course that's 'cause you just keep repeating yourself over and over again. Jim-Sally, Jim-Sally. . . I think your brain might've skipped.

WRITING TO EDIT RECAP

WISK (I'm stepping aside for this one.)

"That sounds like a bunch of hippie . . . dippy . . . baloney." Lord Business in *Lego Movie*. (I told you, I have kids.)

Dialogue Recap

Putting it all together

The age-old, tired-out "show, don't tell" . . . happens to be good advice . . . after you know *how* to show.

Show what your characters are doing through the actions they take. Sometimes your narrator has to *tell* in order to impart information, but it's more engaging to show it.

Examples:

"Jim was annoyed with Sally" is telling. Better to show with "When Sally spoke, Jim frowned down at the eggs in the frying pan."

"Jim didn't want to get the door himself, so he asked Sally" is telling. Better to say, "Sally," Jim said. "Get the door for me, will ya?"

Physical motion—action beats

Remember we talked about the "talking head" syndrome? With action beats, before, during and after someone speaks, you can forgo dialogue tags altogether.

Example:

Jim stared down at the frying pan and watched the spatula slide under the eggs. "Could you close the door for me?"

Shorten up your dialogue.

In real life, people speak in short, choppy sentences and sentence fragments, rather than in long drawn-out sentences with big words. Using contractions—"Let's," "I'll" or "we'd" (we would)—speeds things up and makes dialogue more "real."

Example (And let's combine a couple of these here):

Jim jerked his hand back from the sizzling frying pan. "Dammit," he said, trying not to shout. He clutched his finger. When the door to the kitchen flung open and wind and rain rushed in, he *did* shout, "Could ya get that?" Remembering how Sally was, he quickly calmed down and said, "Please."

Get dialogue tags up front and out early.

A "he said" or "she said" to let the reader know who's speaking.

Bad example:

"Get the door, will ya? That rain's gonna soak the kitchen," Jim said.

Better:

"Could ya get that?" Jim said. "Damn rain's gonna ruin granny's kitchen."

Omit a dialogue tag when it's obvious which character's speaking.

"Sally," Jim said, "could ya get that door?"
"Sure."

Alternative without dialogue tag:

The kitchen door flew open and Jim looked up from the frying pan. "Sally, get that, will ya? Damn rain."

Final Fiction Writing Tips

Don't use passive voice.

Passive—The eggs were busy being fried by Jim.
Active—Jim fried the eggs. Sally stared at his back.

Use a main character as your narrator.

It keeps the pace quicker if you stick with one character's thoughts and perspectives throughout the story. He or she should have no knowledge of the other character's thoughts so we have to show what happens around them. Try to stay in that character's head for most of your novel.

Use omniscient voice when you want to be able to see all and convey all to your reader.

Once you get immersed in writing, stay there.

Scenes unfold best if you're immersed in the world you've created. Characters flow, dialogue's natural, and following the action as it unfolds comes easily for your reader. Let events unfold as they happen and describe them with enough detail that they make sense.

To do that, write for longer stretches of time to stay in your world.

Our dreaded read-through(s)

Read your entire draft in as few sittings as you can. Read out loud as much as you can, especially the dialogue. This will help you figure out if things make sense and the plot flows. It also helps you uncover awkward dialogue.

Keep dialogue tags simple.

Use "said" more often and let the dialogue convey meaning to the reader.

"Get the door!" Jim commanded.

Not as good as:

"Get the door!" Jim shouted.

Or even better:

"Get the door!" Jim said.

Don't let the dialogue tag distract the reader from the dialogue. When readers read the word "said," their mind skips over it. Remember, keep the reader reading by staying out of his or her way. This is why we talked about using "said" instead of "asked."

"Can ya get the door?" Jim said.

Don't "start."

Do not start or begin, just do. (Was that Yoda? He's not in this book, is he?)

Don't have characters "begin" to do something (I'm still guilty of this—I just can't stop). When you say "Jim started stirring the eggs," it's too slow. It doesn't quite get the action going. Just say "Jim stirred the eggs."

The only exception to this is when a character *starting* something is somehow vital to the story.

Jim started the car—the fog on the inside of the windows had finally cleared.

Don't use "as he."

Bad example:

"Jim stirred the eggs, as he thought about Sally the night before."

Better:

"Jim stirred the eggs, thinking of Sally the night before."

Best:

"Jim stirred the eggs and thought about Sally."

In all seriousness, I reference this entire half of the book just about every time I sit down and start writing another novel. I used to have to do that by researching it all over again.

And in the latest update to the cover and a rewrite, I read it again and re-learned more just prior to writing my next fiction novel.

The basics—I read them over and over, practicing. Believe me, it helps.

NEXT STEPS

If you follow what I've laid out in this book, you can and will improve your skills as a self-editing writer. You'll minimize the time it takes to proof your draft before it's sent to an editor.

I wrote this book because I wanted to share what I've learned while writing my stories and editing them successfully.

By learning how to use the basics of fiction dialogue punctuation and transitioning to Scrivener as an editing platform, I've minimized mistakes and sped up the writer-editor process.

The next step's up to you.

The key is to take action. Commit to your novel and your goal of becoming an author. Learn the basics and practice relentlessly.

Decide today that you'll do everything in your power to learn the *mechanics* of storytelling . . . form whatever source you can. (I left that word "form" unedited to remind you that doing it all yourself . . . has risk.)

There's a little gem in everything.

Everything we read as fiction writers, helps us learn and grow and progress our careers. I truly believe that every book has at least one gem that we walk away with, that we wouldn't have found on our own. I know I've tried to pour as many of those in here as I possibly could and when I couldn't, I gave you a place to go find out for yourself.

I bet that the very next time you sit down to write, you'll remember some tips from this book.

You have stories to tell! Learn all you can—learn what works for you.

Do What Works!

Join Us

Stay connected!

Steve Windsor and Lise Cartwright have self-published over 30 titles and that number continues to climb.

They started Author Basics, an author information, training, and community-based support site, for new and aspiring-to-be-great authors.

> "The list of resources that Author Basics continues to churn out is amazing and the community is awesome."

Reasons to join us:

Free Resources - Get your first author freebie, by clicking HERE, or navigating to (https://authorbasics.com/lp1)

Free Community - You can join our awesome author Facebook Group by clicking HERE, or navigating to (https://authorbasics.com/facebook-group)

You can reach us here:
Steve Windsor steve@authorbasics.com
Lise Cartwright at lise@authorbasics.com

The Nine Day Novel Series Continues. . .

The *Nine Day Novel series* continues with this book on editing for fiction writers.

Here's a list of the entire series of *Nine Day Novel* authorship books:

9 Day Novel: Authorphobia
9 Day Novel: Outlining
9 Day Novel: Writing
9 Day Novel: Self-Editing
9 Day Novel: Self-Publishing
9 Day Novel: Book Marketing
9 Day Novel: Writing a Series

Now, go write your novel . . . and make sure you edit it!

ABOUT THE AUTHOR

Steve Windsor was born in Augsburg, Germany to U.S. military parents. So he doesn't know a bit of German.

I'm just a guy who decided to write one day. And roughly two years and approaching two million words into it, I've learned so much and my writing has improved so much. . . But it all came at a cost in time and frustration. I feel like I've bled words.

One of the things I related to a recent interviewer was that if you find the thing that will make you deny sleep, food, bathroom breaks, even sex . . . then that is your true calling. Mine is to write and help other authors learn.

My belief is that I have information you need to avoid some of the frustration and pain that I went through in starting up my dream. And simply put, I want to write books for you because of it.

The fiction I write is hard and raw and my non-fiction is even harder. I don't like to mince words.

I like heroes and villains just about the same, because a good villain usually has a bad backstory that isn't really his or her fault. Sure you gotta kill them, but realize you're going to be a little sad about it, too.

— *Steve Windsor*
Writer, Author, Entrepreneur

Teddy needs your help!

Thank you for reading this book!
I'd love to get your input so I can make the next book in the *Nine Day Novel* series even better.

By now, you realize I'm not above using a baby to promote my books. And "Teddy" is hard at work in my sweatshop, writing reviews and posting to Facebook for me.

Help Teddy out. Every review this book gets I give Teddy a day off. Click HERE and give Teddy a day off.

He thanks you. . .